CONURES • SILVA & KOTLAR

ISBN 0-87666-893-7 • KW-121

CONTENTS

PHOTO CREDITS
Front cover shows a Queen of Bavaria conure, *Aratinga guarouba*, photographed by the San Diego Zoo. The back cover shows a nan-day conure, *Nandayus nenday,* photographed by Dr. Herbert R. Axelrod. The frontispiece shows a halfmoon conure. The front end-pages show model Thomas Arthur Cuccurullo with his pet nanday conure. Photos by Dr. Herbert R. Axelrod. The back endpages show (page 95) an orange-fronted conure, *Aratinga canicularis clarae,* and (page 94) a Mexican or green conure, *Aratinga h. holochlora.* Photos by Dr. Herbert R. Axelrod and the San Diego Zoo.

Distributed in the U.S. by T.F.H. Publications, Inc., 211 West Sylvania Avenue, PO Box 427, Neptune, NJ 07753; in England by T.F.H. (Gt. Britain) Ltd., 13 Nutley Lane, Reigate, Surrey; in Canada to the pet trade by Rolf C. Hagen Ltd., 3225 Sartelon Street, Montreal 382, Quebec; in Southeast Asia by Y.W. Ong, 9 Lorong 36 Geylang, Singapore 14; in Australia and the South Pacific by Pet Imports Pty. Ltd.. P.O. Box 149, Brookvale 2100, N.S.W. Australia; in South Africa by Valid Agencies, P.O. Box 51901, Randburg 2125 South Africa. Published by T.F.H. Publications, Inc., Ltd, the British Crown Colony of Hong Kong.

CONURES

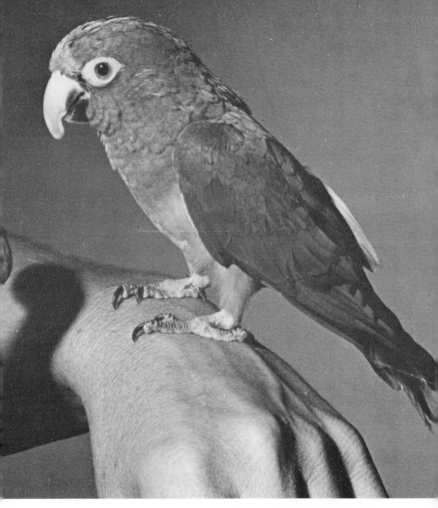

TONY SILVA
and
BARBARA KOTLAR

Conures are becoming increasingly popular as pets because of their intelligence and beauty. They are tame and affectionate, characteristics which endear them to bird owners. Conures are found in many sizes and colors, from large Patagonians which grow to about twenty inches to the painted variety which grow no higher than nine inches. Conures range in color from a lush green to a highly coveted brilliant yellow. Red, blue, orange, brown and white all serve to highlight the beautiful feathering of the conure.

The conure is a smaller version of the macaw; its shape is slender, and its tail is tapered and graduated. Dr. Matthew Vriends, the leading Dutch authority on these birds, demonstrates (facing page) how easy they are to handle. In the lower photo, Dr. Vriends poses to give the reader a better idea of the size of a mature nanday conure. Photos by Dr. Herbert R. Axelrod.

Conures generally belong to the genus *Aratinga*. Their natural habitat ranges from Mexico and Central America to the Caribbean Islands and South America. Many varieties of the conures still live in the wild, usually in flocks, but as civilization encroaches, more and more of the birds are becoming scarce, and some varieties are even on the brink of extinction.

The conure is a smaller version of the macaw; its shape is slender, and its tail is tapered and graduated. Its eye ring is usually bare, but the rest of the facial area is fully feathered. The harsh screech of the conure points to the fact that this mighty little bird deserves as much attention from the pet world as does the macaw. Most will learn a few words; however, the conure is not an excellent mimic. Its voice is high-pitched and unclear. Despite its speaking limitations, there is no denying that the conure is a noisy bird.

A golden-capped conure in front of the nestbox in which it breeds. Conures are relatively easy to breed.

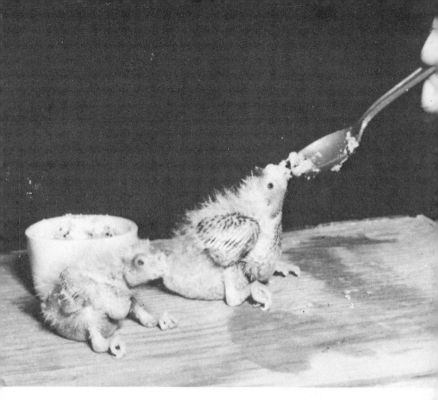

Young cockatiels being hand-raised. Hand-feeding baby birds is not difficult. Get the book *Hand-feeding Baby Birds* if you think you may need the expertise.

The conure is relatively easy to breed, a very desirable characteristic. Once breeding is established, the conure will breed year after year, making the conure much sought after in the avicultural world. They are hardy birds, rarely becoming sick, but even though the conure can survive on minimal care, reasonable precautions should be taken in maintaining the bird.

This book deals with the different kinds of conures and their characteristics. It explains everything from purchasing, caging and caring for the birds to breeding the conure and hatching the eggs. Finally, diseases that are common to the parrot world will be discussed. It is the authors' hope that the book will add to the knowledge and understanding of the remarkable conure.

The photo above shows a pair of jan-day conures, *Aratinga jandaya.* They are found mostly in eastern Brazil. Photo by Walsrode Birdpark. On the right is the rare Patagonian conure, also called the burrowing parrot, *Cyanoliseus patagonus.* It grows to about 18 inches. Photo by P. Leyser.

Kinds of Conures

There are many different varieties of conures that belong to the genus *Aratinga,* but it is not within the scope of this book to discuss all of them. Only those that are most likely to be available in pet shops will be described.

Nanday Conure *(Nandayus nenday)*

This conure actually belongs to the genus *Nandayus,* but because of its close resemblance to the members of *Aratinga,* it is usually grouped with the conures. The nanday's head and beak are black, the body is green, the throat

and breast are blue, and there is red on the feet which are a brownish pink. The wings are blue-black, and the tail feathers are gray. The immature birds have smaller, less colorful bodies.

The nanday has proven to be a willing breeder in captivity and has even crossed with other conures, including the janday conure. It can be easily tamed, thereby making it a lovable pet. It can learn to speak a few words, but it is not a clear mimic.

The nanday has a length of 12 in. Its native setting includes Bolivia, Paraguay, Brazil and Argentina.

Gold-Crown Conure *(Aratinga aurea aurea)*

This bird is sometimes called the peach-fronted conure. It reaches a length of 10½ in. It is found predominately in Brazil, and another subspecies is found in Bolivia, Paraguay and Argentina.

The feathers on the body are green and the forehead is a yellow-orange. The bird has a feathered orange eye ring. The bill and feet are black, and traces of blue can be found on the head and tail feathers. The immatures have lighter bills, and there is less orange on the head. This bird is not as noisy as some of the conures. Often it is unwilling to nest, but when it does, this conure is a constant breeder. If taught at an early age, the gold-crown conure becomes a good mimic with a clear strong voice.

Halfmoon Conure *(Aratinga canicularis eburnirostrum)*

The halfmoon conure is a subspecies of *Aratinga canicularis,* the orange-fronted conure. It generally grows to about 9 in. A very popular and plentiful bird, the halfmoon has a green body with an orange forehead, and the bare skin around the eye is light orange-yellow. The crown is a dull blue and the bill is horn-colored. Immatures have dark brown irises and less orange on the forehead. This conure

The scarlet-fronted conure, *Aratinga wagleri*. Photo by Louise Van der Meid. Photo courtesy of *Parrots and Related Birds*, by Bates and Busenbark.

The peach-fronted conure, *Aratinga aurea aurea,* is also called the gold-crowned conure, a name we prefer. These two views of the same bird were photographed by Dr. Herbert R. Axelrod.

14

The reddish-bellied conure, *Pyrrhura frontalis*. Photo by Harry Lacey.

originates from the western sections of Central America and Mexico and, consequently, is a common bird in Mexican markets.

Brown-Throated Conure *(Aratinga pertinax)*

There are at least thirteen subspecies of *Aratinga pertinax,* the main difference between them being the amount of orange displayed on the head area. The bird has a black beak and feet and a green body with lighter feathering underneath. There is brown on the chest and, in some subspecies, on the cheek. Its length is 10 in.

The brown-throated conure makes a good pet and can learn to speak a few words. It is said to be a good breeder; however, the authors have never owned any that went to nest.

Its natural habitat is the offshore islands of Venezuela and northern South America. One of its most attractive subspecies, in which the orange continues onto the crown of the head, is found on Bonaire, also the home of the yellow-shouldered Amazon. The brown-throated conure has been introduced to St. Thomas, but the population there is not large. A friend who visits the island frequently states the birds are very destructive and are often shot.

Dusky Conure *(Aratinga weddellii)*

Only recently has the dusky conure, which originates in western South America, been offered in large numbers in the pet world.

The dusky conure is not very attractive, but it is, nevertheless, desirable as a pet. Its body is green, the head a gray-brown, the tips of the feathers on the crown have a blue cast and the legs are gray. The bird grows to a length of 11 in.

Sun Conure *(Aratinga solstitialis)*

This golden beauty is an excellent breeder in captivity, and many captive-raised birds are offered for sale yearly.

Above: Nandays become tame and affectionate. Their voice is very high-pitched and somewhat unclear. Below: Brown-throated conures are frequently available because they are so easily bred in captivity. Photos by Tony Silva.

Above: This ivory conure, recently imported, shows the wear and tear a long trip has on a conure. Spray daily with a fine mist of water and the plumage will quickly grow in. Below: A blue-headed conure. Photos by Tony Silva.

The only undesirable trait the bird has is its noisy behavior. It screeches loudly when alarmed, but it is a great mimic and easily learns to talk. It makes a charming pet and commands a good price when offered for sale.

The bird has gold-orange plumage on its body with wings and a tail of green. In the immatures gold is mixed with the green. The feet and beak are black. The sun grows to 12 in. The bird comes from the Guianas, Brazil and Venezuela. Crosses between the sun and janday conures, with the name of Sunday, are often offered on the market.

Janday Conure *(Aratinga jandaya)*

This bird is probably the most available of the conures. It is closely related to the sun conures and the golden-capped conures. Its yellow head blends into red in the belly area, the wings and back are green, and the beak and feet are black. The immatures are duller in color.

The janday can be sexed easily by observing the color of the eyes. The iris of the female is a light brown and the skin around the eye is a grayish white. In the male the iris is darker and the skin around the eye is a pure white. This observation is not 100% accurate, but it has been noted in breeding pairs and surgically sexed birds. It grows to the length of 12 in.

The janday conure is an active bird, besides being a noisemaker and a great chewer. As a pet, it is tame and lovable. Its native home is northeastern Brazil, but as more land clearance occurs, the range of this bird decreases.

Golden-Capped Conure *(Aratinga auricapilla)*

This conure has been offered only recently on the market. It is often available in pet shops now since many breedings have occurred in captivity.

The golden-capped conure grows to a length of 12 in. The orange-red on its forehead and chest is set off by its green body plumage and its black beak and feet.

The janday conure, *Aratinga jandaya*, is probably the most readily available of all the conures. They are easily sexed by the color of the eyes. The iris of the female is light brown while the male has a darker iris and has white skin around the eye. Photo by Harry Lacey.

Quaker conures, shown above and below, are the least expensive of all conures. They are also noisy and destructive. Photos by Tony Silva.

Above: A young pair of slender bill conures. Below: Golden-capped conures are a frequent import even though they are easily bred. Tony Silva photos.

A pair of cactus conures, *Aratinga cactorum*. Photo by Walsrode Birdpark.

The bird is not as beautiful as the sun or janday, but it is still an attractive specimen. Unfortunately, those in the authors' collection are shy and prefer to hide most of the day. The golden-capped conure comes from the forest of eastern Brazil, and even though much of the dense forest is being removed for farming and grazing cattle, the bird is not yet on the endangered species list.

White-eye or Green Conure
(Aratinga leucopthalmus)
This large (13 in.) conure is mostly green except for a few specks of red on the head and the underwings which are red and yellow. It has a horn-colored beak, gray feet and a white eye ring. The immatures lack the red and yellow under the wings.

This conure is tame and gentle by nature. It speaks clearly and is very intelligent, doing tricks and rolling over on command, if taught. It ranges over most of South America, and, consequently, many of these birds are offered for sale at a reasonable price.

Mitred Conure (Aratinga mitrata)
This is a very beautiful bird closely related to other conures which have red on the forehead and green on the body. The mitred's beak is horn-colored, its feet are brown and it grows to a length of 15 in. The immatures, however, have less red on the forehead and dark irises.

The mitred conure is both intelligent and noisy. It will learn to talk easily and will become fairly tame as well as breed readily. Western South America is its native area.

Finsch's Conure (Aratinga finschi)
This conure is smaller (11 in.) than the mitred and not as beautiful. It has a green body with red on its forehead, horn-colored mandibles and a pronounced white ring

Above: Nanday conures. The females have smaller and slimmer heads than the males. Photo by Tony Silva. On the facing page is the peach-fronted conure. Photo by Dr. Herbert R. Axelrod.

around the eye. The immatures have a dark iris and lack the red on the forehead.

This bird originates in Nicaragua, Costa Rica and Panama but is not readily available to the bird fancier. Finsch's conure makes an excellent pet, being both lovable and easily trained.

Cherry-Headed Conure *(Aratinga erythrogenys)*

This beauty has been recently available in large numbers. It has a green body with red around the head and on the wings. The eye ring is yellow and the feet are gray. The immature has gray eyes and lacks red on the head.

The bird is easy to tame and quickly learns to talk. One pet cherry-headed conure the authors are acquainted with dances and will flap its wings on command. The bird comes from Peru and Ecuador, where it is so plentiful that the natives will catch the birds and raise them as pets.

Blue-Crowned Conure *(Aratinga acuticaudata)*

This conure has a green body with a blue cast to its head. In the authors' collection the females have smaller heads that are a duller blue. The immature lacks any blue on its forehead. The beak is long and pointed with a black color that turns lighter at the tip. The blue-crowned conure is a fairly large bird, growing to a length of 15 in.

The blue-crowned conure can be likened to a smaller version of a macaw in its behavior—it is noisy and often temperamental. Two blue-crowned conures that have been observed have chewed the bottom of their box while incubating. The bird's native range includes Colombia, Venezuela and Argentina.

Painted Conure *(Pyrrhura picta)*

This beautiful conure is now available occasionally, and it is used for breeding in captivity. The adult has a green body with the crown, upper breast, neck, throat and cheeks

A cherry-headed conure, *Aratinga erythrogenys,* is a popular and expensive conure because it is easily tamed and quickly learns to talk. Photo by Louise Van der Meid.

To the left is a golden-capped conure, *Aratinga auricapilla,* photo by P. Leyser. Above is an underside view of the gold-crowned conure, *A. aurea.* On the facing page is a peach-fronted conure, a different subspecies of *A. aurea.* Photos by Barbara Kotlar and Dr. Herbert R. Axelrod.

The Patagonian conure, *Cyanoliseus patagonus* is a very rare and unusually colored parrot. It is an endangered species in its range in South America, so few are available to aviculturists who might well succeed in breeding them as they have other endangered species. As a matter of fact there are probably a dozen species of parrots which are more plentiful as pets than they a brown color. The chest and rump are red and the tail maroon. There is white on the ears and the fringe of the feathers on the throat. The wings are green with red at the bend, and the beak is black like the feet. It will grow to a length of 9 in.

Patagonian Conure *(Cyanoliseus patagonus)*

This conure is a favorite for its beauty and size, growing to a length of 18 in. The bill is often hidden by cheek feathers. The head, wings, tail and upper part of the body arebrown; yellow and red are featured on the lower abdomen.

Slender-Billed Conure
(Enicognathus leptorhynchus)

This bird's native habitats are Chile and Chiloe Island. It is a large bird, 16 in., with a dull green body color. The feathers are edged with a dull brown; the abdomen has brownish red on it, as does the tail; the head is a lighter green than the body. It is also characterized by brown legs and a black overgrown beak. The males have less red on the belly, a larger, darker green head and a curved bill. Females have smaller heads, more red on the belly and the pelvic bones are further apart. In males these may touch, while in females there is a greater space between them.

The immatures are like adults, but the plumage is a darker green, and the short bill is tipped in horn color. The iris is darker, and the feet are much smoother and slightly lighter in color.

Slender-billed conures are not endangered, but they are suffering from habitat destruction, shooting and persecution as pests. They prove willing breeders; captive-raised birds appear to breed fairly easily and regularly. Slender-bill conures are not common, but some are imported yearly. These birds have suffered from exotic Newcastles disease, which could also be a cause of the decrease in numbers.

On the facing page is the Cuban conure, *Aratinga euops*. To the right is a color photo of the same picture as that on page 24, the cactus conure, while below is the jandaya conure. Photos by Dr. Herbert R. Axelrod.

Cactus Conure *(Aratinga cactorum)*

The cactus conure grows to a length of 10 in. Its native habitat is northwestern Brazil. Brown is present on the forehead and upper breast, the back of the head and wings is green, the lower chest is orange-yellow and the feet and beak are gray. Recently this bird has been made available by several importers. It is a good breeder and is said to make a good pet.

Aztec Conure *(Aratinga nana astec)*

This little Mexican conure grows to a length of 10 in. and it is often available on the market. The beautiful Aztec conure has a green head, back and wings. The chest is brown; the feet and beak are gray. Its small size makes it attractive to those bird fanciers who are considering a small pet.

Queen of Bavaria Conure *(Aratinga guarouba)*

This Brazilian conure is the most sought after of all the conures. It is extremely rare and therefore very expensive. Since it is also listed as endangered, it is protected by international law.

The plumage on the Queen of Bavaria conure is yellow. The primaries are green on this brilliantly colored conure, the beak is horn-colored and the feet are pink. In captivity, this bird rarely flies; rather it climbs. It is extremely noisy and active, and often the Queen of Bavaria conure has a tendency to pluck its wing and chest feathers. A small cage makes a suitable place for breeding. Here in the United States one exceptional pair has produced over twenty young.

Cuban Conure *(Aratinga euops)*

This rare and very beautiful conure is green with red speckles on its head and upper chest. The beak is horn-colored, and the feet are gray. The Cuban conure can be confused with the white-eye conure and is often advertised as such. Unfortunately it is noisy, but it makes a good pet.

It is rarely offered for sale, but recently it has been available in Europe where it is being bred. This conure has become rare in Cuba where it is called *Catey* and *Periquitos.*

Blue-Throated Conure *(Pyrrhura cruentata)*

This is the largest of the *Pyrrhura* conures and one of the most beautiful. This bird is included in a class with the Queen of Bavaria conure because it is rare and endangered. Since the Queen of Bavaria is being raised in the United States, there is hope to save that bird from extinction, but this is not the case with the blue-throated conure. The only way to save this species is through captive breeding. Pyrrhura conures produce large clutches in captivity and also prove willing nesters, so there is hope of saving this bird. The habitat of this conure is Minas Gerais, Brazil, which is an area that has been cleared extensively in recent years.

The blue-throated conure has a green body. Its rump is red, it has black feathers on the head and the tail is tan. The conure also has green cheeks, a blue throat and there is red on the abdomen. It has a brown beak and feet.

Austral Conure *(Enicognathus ferrugineus)*

This bird is also known as the Magellan conure. Along with the slender-billed conure, this is the only parrot exported from Chile. The Patagonian conure that is found there is protected.

This bird produces large clutches, and a few are now being raised in the States. It is green with a maroon tail, has a brown-black beak, gray feet and a brown-colored forehead. The austral conure grows to about 13 in. and is found in lower Argentina as well as Chile. It is the most southerly distributed parrot, being found in the Tierra del Fuego. This conure will scratch its head and cere with a claw if left alone as a pet (this was observed in the authors' collection). Drafts or a drop in temperature will affect the bird, which seems unusual since it comes from an area that has freezing temperatures.

When purchasing your bird, be sure that you carefully inspect your conure. Look closely at the feathers. A clipped wing or broken tail, as shown on the facing page, is not important the feathers are strong and healthy. Examine the feathers closely and be alert for any parasites, rashes on the skin under the feathers or blood feather Photos by Dr. Herbert R. Axelrod.

Purchasing
a
Bird

When purchasing a bird, make certain the supplier is reliable and that the bird has been well cared for. This should be the foremost consideration. The intermediate habitat should be clean, and the birds should not be over-crowded.

Look carefully at the bird's eyes and nostrils. They should be free of discharge, redness and inflammation. The beak should be smooth with no cracks in it. Except for the slender-billed conure, the beak should not be overgrown. The vent should be clean, not swollen or stained. The chest

On the facing page is the rare olive-throated or Jamaican conure, while the photo above shows a white-eared conure. Photos by Dr. Herbert R. Axelrod and Louise Van der Meid.

must not be bald or feather-picked but it should be round and full. If the chest appears sunken or the breastbone sticks out, this is an indication that the bird is sick and not feeding. The bird should be breathing evenly with no sign of congestion. A broken tail or clipped wings should not be viewed as undesirable when purchasing a bird.

If it is possible, hold the conure on your finger to see if it firmly grips it. If not, this might indicate a broken leg. Beware if the bird is missing more than one toe or nail. Scaly feet can mean the bird is old. The waste material should be firm with green droppings and white urine, not watery, red, black or soupy green.

Carefully observe the above characteristics of the bird and its behavior. The conure that is relatively calm when approached by strangers will most likely be the easiest to tame since it is not afraid or shy. It is more pleasurable and perhaps profitable to purchase a healthy and happy conure than one that might have problems.

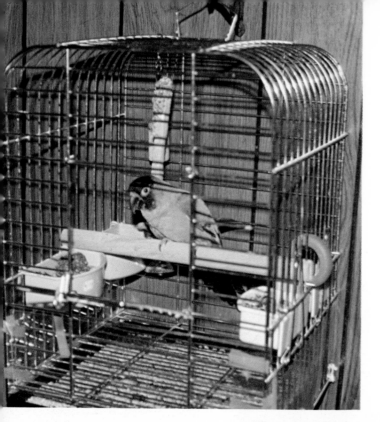

Conures' cages, shown above, should always be clean and airy. Leg bands, shown to the right, are required for imported birds going through quarantine. Photos by Barbara Kotlar.

General Maintenance

CAGING

The cage should be large enough so that the bird's head does not touch the top of the cage and its tail does not hit the bottom. The conure must be able to move freely inside its confinement. If breeding is a goal for the bird fancier, the pair must have ample room in the cage. The authors' slender-billed conures are housed in a cage 2' x 2' x 3' where they have bred successfully for the past couple of years. Parrot-type birds do not need a high flight for breeding. Many successes have been reported in cages and very small flights.

There should be two perches in the cage — one up high for the bird to roost at night and one near water, food and gravel cups. The perches and cups should be kept clean at all times. The bottom of the cage should be lined with either newspaper, which should be removed daily to keep the cage clean or bedding, such as ground corn cob or pine shavings which are absorbent. The latter scatters, though, when the bird flaps its wings.

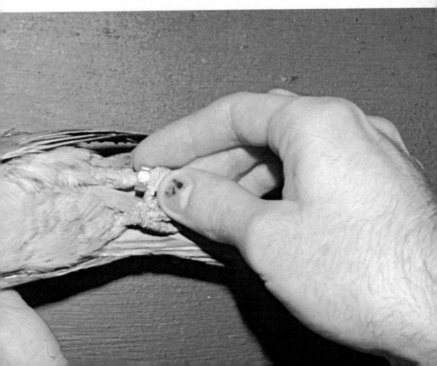

Toys are enjoyed by many birds, distracting them from boredom and loneliness. Artificial bones and metal bells are only a few that are on the market. Plastic and wood are two materials that conures enjoy destroying, and it is not uncommon for the conure to chew its own perch.

Never leave a conure out of its cage unless it is supervised. If the bird is frightened and takes flight, it might fly into some object or window, injuring itself.

If the cage is placed in the kitchen, there is a possibility that the bird might be affected by fumes, especially those of burnt Teflon. Never place a cage in a draft, for this is the number one killer of birds. The cage should not be directly in front of a heat or air-conditioning vent. Covering the cage at night is not a necessity, but it is most appreciated by the bird since it affords the conure a sense of security. If utilizing a large flight, provide the bird with some protection. If the cage is placed in the sun, cover part of it so the bird can sit in the shade if it so desires.

To keep the bird in good health be sure its surroundings are kept clean. Do not use spray paints or other materials whose vapors can be harmful in the same area where the bird is. Twigs that are given to the bird should be nonpoisonous; apple and pear branches are safe, not cherry. Exercise the bird daily. It will enjoy the session as much as the owner. Finally, a bird should never be abused. Keep children from poking at the cage or pulling at the bird's feathers. An incident like this could ruin a bird's disposition for life. Above all, enjoy the bird, for it wants to return the same affection it receives.

FEEDING

In the wild, conures and other parrot-type birds feed mainly on nuts, seeds, fruit, vegetables and berries. Since wild birds get a great deal of exercise, this diet affords all the nutrients essential for good health. However, a bird that leads a more sedentary life, such as a pet bird, should be on a restricted diet. Sunflower seeds, fruit and other seeds, such as safflower, should be the main staples. Peanuts, dry corn, monkey chow, dry dog food and vegetables can also be added. Recommended fruits and vegetables include carrots, corn on the cob, apples, pears, oranges, grapes, endive and sweet potatoes. If possible, use five or more kinds a day.

Raw vegetables and fruit are preferable. If cooked, do not add a flavor enhancer. Instead, sprinkle the vegetables with vitamins and the fruit with wheat germ or cod-liver oil. There is also a parrot mix readily available in pet shops. Do not feed the bird table scraps. Not only is it bad for the bird, but the conure will also most certainly become spoiled and become a nuisance by screeching at mealtime. Only a couple of peanuts should be given daily since they are high in fat content. Have food available for the bird at all times. However, do not allow food to spoil in the cage. Wash the food containers regularly with hot water.

Safflower seeds are now becoming a popular substitute and supplement for sunflower seeds, which some breeders claim are addictive. One breeder maintains his birds on safflower which he says keep them more active, healthier and in better plumage.

Conures and other parrot-like birds enjoy hard-boiled egg yolk, which should only be fed occasionally. A special treat can be a cooked chicken drumstick which has been stripped of most of its meat. The bird will ravenously chew the gristle on the joint. A cooked round steak bone will become a popular item, as will chicken, lean beef and young lamb which can be given now and then. A bird is known to kill mice if it has the opportunity, so feeding it meat occasionally will not harm the bird.

Vitamins can also be added to the bird's drinking water as well as to the food. Fresh water must be provided daily, and the cup must be thoroughly cleaned. Cod-liver oil and multi-vitamins which include vitamin A can be purchased at any pet shop.

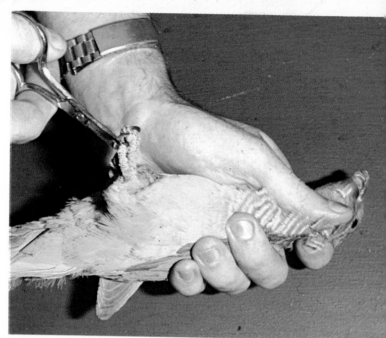

Clipping the claws on a quaker. Below: An ordinary scissors will do in clipping a conure's wing (gold-crowned conure). On the facing page is an ideal conure cage which has plenty of room. Photos by Barbara Kotlar and Tony Silva.

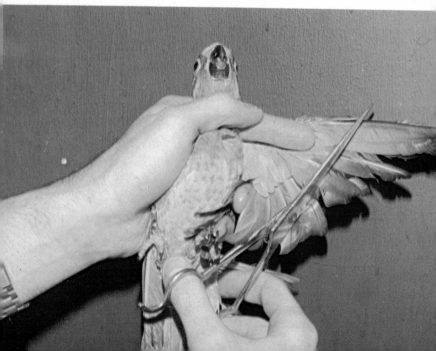

Gravel or oyster shell should be kept in a separate cup. This will help the conure in the task of grinding and breaking seeds since the bird has no teeth. Cuttlebones can be given, but the bird most likely will rip it to pieces in a short time.

Unflavored gelatin is an excellent source of protein to add to the conure's diet. It should be softened in cold water, and wheat germ and cereal can then be mixed in to form a paste. To make this even more palatable, a peanut or two can be added.

Recently, several bird foods in the form of pellets have appeared on the market. Some are artificially colored red which supposedly attracts the bird's attention more readily. If this food is used, be sure to supplement it with fresh fruit, seeds and nuts, since alone it cannot provide all the nutrients necessary to maintain the bird in top physical condition. If the bird is fed just one type of food, it soon loses interest in eating and becomes bored. Variety is the spice of life not only to humans but also to the fine-feathered friends of the world.

BATHING

In the wild a parrot will bathe by holding its wings open to catch the drops of rain. Sometimes it will rub itself against wet foliage, as observed in the Cuban amazon.

Bathing will keep the plumage glossy and beautiful. Daily spraying will help feathering that is ragged or frayed. The bird can be sprayed with warm water from a plastic bottle designed for misting plants. Often the bird will enjoy this so much it will open its wings completely to get a thorough cleansing.

Some birds are inclined to take a complete bath. Often by running an electric appliance, such as a food chopper, the bird will become agitated sufficiently to take a bath. If this is the case, provide the conure with a shallow bowl of warm water. The bird will step in it and clean itself by throwing water up with its beak. Be sure the cage or area where it is bathing is not in a draft. Towel dry the bird or use a portable hair dryer with the setting low and held at least a foot from the bird. It is a good idea for the bird to take its bath in the morning so it will have the rest of the day to completely dry.

There will be a great deal of preening the feathers after the bath. The bird will reach down to its oil gland, located at the tail end of its body, and take the oil to lubricate its feathers, thereby giving itself a beautiful sheen.

GROOMING

The nails should be clipped regularly by removing the tips. Use the nail clippers available for small dogs. Avoid cutting in too deep. If in doubt, just clip a little at a time, but if bleeding does occur, apply an antiseptic powder. File the nails to remove sharp edges. After the nails are clipped, the owner will find it more comfortable when the bird perches on his hand.

CLIPPING BEAKS

A beak which is overgrown can easily be clipped. A clipper used for trimming the toenails of dogs is most suitable for this task. There is a blood vein that is present in the beak and care must be taken that the beak is not overcut so that bleeding occurs. If the vein is cut into, use hydrogen peroxide to help coagulate the blood. Otherwise, after the tip is cut, file the rest of the beak down to normal size with an emery board.

In the wild few birds have overgrown beaks. In captivity, however, the bird might not have enough objects at its disposal to chew. As the caged bird grows older, its beak can become more of a problem, often making it even difficult for the bird to eat. If the bird is not tame enough for the owner to perform the task of clipping the beak, take the bird to a qualified veterinarian or pet shop handler who has experience along this line.

Left: One way to hold a conure for inspection. The head must be held securely or the bird will bite you. On the facing, page a nanday conure has been tamed, and now he is being trained to climb on a finger. Photos by Barbara Kotlar and Dr. Herbert R. Axelrod.

Taming

An owner is fortunate if he obtains a bird that has already been tamed or at least is not afraid of humans. Some birds allow a person to hand-feed them, which is very desirable. Naturally, these birds command a higher price. When approaching a strange bird, never offer a finger. Offer the back of a closed hand. This will show the bird the tamer is not afraid of it and will lessen the possibility of getting bitten. If a bird does bite a finger, push the finger into the bird's mouth, not away. The bird will bite the whole finger this way and not just a small portion which may result in a deep v-shaped cut. Never hit the bird. This will destroy all future trust between the owner and the bird.

Taming the bird can be a rewarding adventure, just as teaching the bird to talk. A bird that is tame is more of a pleasure to own and will make a better pet, since it has lost its fear of man. Taming small birds, such as conures, love-birds and cockatiels, is a simple task but requires some time.

Some people are more successful in taming birds than others. It is important that the person is not afraid of the bird. Fear can be sensed by the bird, which will make it impossible for a workable relationship to develop.

First of all, a wing or wings should be clipped. One is preferable, as it will keep the bird permanently grounded. Some birds will fly well with both wings clipped. If a bird escapes its confines, it can fly into objects and become injured. Clipping a wing is not a cruel act. The feathers will grow back in approximately six months. If the bird is to become a pet and live in a human environment, precautions must be taken to help it safely adapt to its new surroundings.

Most likely, the bird's wing will have already been clipped when purchased, but if this is not the case, do the following. Clip the primary flight feathers, that is, the first seven to eight feathers, on one wing, to the second row of feathers or wing coverts.

If you are hesitant about clipping the wings or the bird will not allow you to do so, call a pet shop to ask if it can be of assistance. It is also a good idea to find a vet that has had some experience with birds in case his medical knowledge is needed.

A bathroom makes a good working area for taming the bird. Place the bird on a perch. If it insists on flying off, keep on picking the bird up and placing it on the perch again and again until the conure becomes accustomed to staying on it. Once this is accomplished, place another perch next to the bird and push the bird on the chest to get it to step up to the other perch. This is called a ladder trick.

Continue until the conure steps up without hesitation. Do this twice a day. Next, try to substitute a finger. If the bird attempts to bite, blow on it. It will soon learn to behave. The bird can be rewarded with a piece of fruit, nut or cracker. Speak lovingly to the bird so it knows it has won your approval when successfully performing this trick.

It is easy to teach a bird to pick up its foot. Just touch the foot so the bird picks it up. Say, "Pick up a foot." Try it several times a day. The bird will soon learn what the owner expects of it. Reward and praise the bird. This will keep it interested and willing to learn new tricks.

Learning to play dead sounds more difficult than it really is. The bird is held bodily and given a twig or perch to grab. Slowly place it on its back. If the bird resists, try again. Once the bird realizes it is not in danger, it will trust the owner to place it in this position. If the bird won't co-operate, place one of its feet on the other and turn the bird on its back. Talk slowly and calmly to soothe the bird. Push its head back gently so it appears the bird is dead. It might take several weeks before this trick is learned.

A bird can be taught to pick up an object and bring it to the owner. Place the bird on a table and give it a key. Have the bird walk to you by offering it a treat. If the bird carries the key and drops it in front of the trainer, reward it. The bird will catch on quickly to what is expected of it.

The effort put into taming the bird is well worthwhile. The bird will trust its owner and will allow itself to be handled. A special bond will arise between owner and pet which will prove to be beneficial should the bird ever become ill and have to be nursed. However, it should be noted that just because a bird has been tamed by one person does not mean it will cooperate with another. There are many one-person birds, and beware to anyone else who might try to handle the bird.

Teaching
the
Conure
to Talk

Actually, a parrot-type bird cannot talk; it only mimics sounds. For clarification purposes, the word "talk" will be used for mimic. The conure can be taught to talk before it is trained, and wild birds do learn to talk as well as captive-bred birds.

There are several approaches in this undertaking. First of all, the tamer and younger the bird is, the easier it will be to train. A bird learns through repetition of sounds, so there should be no distractions in a training session. Set aside a certain period of time daily—two short training sessions are

You can hardly teach a conure to talk unless it learns to mimic your voice. It doesn't have to be tame to do this, but it helps. First clip the wings (below) and then handle it (facing page) as much as possible. Photos by Dr. Herbert R. Axelrod.

If you want your conure to talk (mimic), only one person should have the responsibility of teaching it. There are several tapes and records available from your petshop to help you train your conure to speak (mimic), but your own voice is just as good if you follow sound principles in training your pet conure. Photo by Dr. Herbert R. Axelrod.

more beneficial than one long one. Only one person should have the responsibility of teaching the bird to talk. Otherwise, confusion arises, often frustrating the bird as well as the owner. Use a simple word when talking to the bird and repeat, repeat, repeat. This is the key. At first, the sounds from the bird will be indistinct, more of a muttering. Gradually, they will become clearer.

There are several records and tapes available if the owner does not want to undertake the training session himself. The record must be played for several weeks before results can be heard. Once a bird learns its first sound, others can be learned more easily.

It is a good idea to repeat the word "water" when fresh water is placed in the cage or the word "fruit" when a piece is given, etc. This might enable the bird to associate the sound with the object. Although it is generally known that birds only mimic sounds, association with words is a trait observed by many bird owners. One of the authors' maroon-belly conures will say "water" when it starts its bath. A nanday conure will ask for "fruit" if it is missing from its cage.

Parrots are known to be teachers themselves. It is not unusual for a bird to pick up sounds another bird makes. A bird will also learn to bark like a dog if there is one to learn from.

If the bird owner is really serious about teaching his bird, the following method might prove useful to him. Place the bird in a dark room on a stand. Light a candle in the middle of the room and sit comfortably. Repeat the word clearly for at least ten minutes. The bird will not be distracted and will be listening intently. Two sessions a day are recommended. It is hoped that the bird will be talking in a short period of time.

Often the owner will give up before the bird learns to talk. Patience and perseverance are necessary when dealing with parrot-type birds.

To the left is a red-bellied conure, *Pyrrhura frontalis*. Photo
Walsrode Birdpark. Below, a
gold-crowned conure is being
held preparatory to its wings
ing clipped. Photo by Barbara
Kotlar.

Breeding

58

Many rare, threatened and endangered species are now being captive-raised and bred to insure their survival. Most birds are becoming rare because of habitat destruction or persecution for ruination of crops, not because of the pet trade. Aviculturists have established many species since some countries have prohibited the exportation of their wildlife. The turquoisine and scarlet-chested parakeets, both endangered, are now more common in captivity than in the wild. At present there are only two conures endangered—the Queen of Bavaria and the blue-throated conures. However, breeders must be encouraged to breed all conures to enable all varieties to firmly establish themselves in a controlled environment.

The most difficult problem that faces the breeder is obtaining birds of the opposite sex. Few parrots are sexually dimorphic. A new method is available for determining the sex of a bird, but the operation carries a small risk since the bird is given an anesthetic. A small incision is made on the side of the bird, and an endoscope is inserted. The sex of the bird is revealed and also the approximate age, health and breeding condition. In some birds the sex can be determined by observing the color of the irises—females have red while the males are black. Several birds also have differences in the color of their plumage. Some breeders maintain that the head and beak of a male are larger than the female's. The pelvic bones are often closer in the male and further apart in the female. The most natural method of obtaining a pair is to buy several birds and let them choose a mate. Of course, this is costly and sometimes risky, for a bird can be injured or killed by another.

Once the owner is relatively certain he has a pair, a suitable cage or flight for breeding should be set up. Slender-billed conures breed very well in a small cage. However, some breeders prefer large flights. The screening must be small and double wired, or the birds might be injured and lose a toe. A small nesting box should be placed in or attached to the cage. *Pyrrhura* and *Aratinga* conures can be kept in a cockatiel nesting box—12" x 12" x 12". If a nesting box is used, it should be wired on the inside to protect the wood from the conure. A door or cover should be built into the box in case the eggs or chicks must be removed. Metal boxes or small garbage cans are also used successfully. However, these must never be placed in the sun since they quickly become hot. Some breeders prefer to use a natural log that has been cleaned and treated with a mite and lice spray and hollowed enough for the bird to get inside. Most birds will chew the log to their liking. The nesting box should be placed in the highest spot in the cage or aviary to give the bird a sense of security. Pine, sawdust

A pair of scarlet-fronted conures. Photos by Louise Van der Meid.

This series of photos shows the development of two slender bill conure chicks. The photo above if of 18-day-olds. The lower photo is one day later.

The slender bill conure chicks shown above are 21 days old, while the chicks shown below are 24 days old. They are being hand-fed by the author.

Some breeders believe in the use of seed sprouts for feeding breeders. Just put some bird seed into a shallow aluminum pan, add water and cover with a damp towel. In a few days it will begin to sprout as shown above (one week) and below (4 days). Photos by Dr. Herbert R. Axelrod.

or shavings, which can include peat and other materials, are used to fill two-thirds of the inside of the boxes. In hot and dry climates the pine should be soaked since it will aid the chick in picking its way out of the egg. The inside and outside of the box, as well as the floor of the aviary, can also be misted. The humidity should be kept at 50-55% for best results. Bathing water should be provided as well, since parrots will often take a bath a few days before the eggs are due to hatch.

Birds must first adapt themselves to their surroundings before they will breed. Once established many will breed continuously for years. It is not necessary to have more than one pair, since parrots do not need the stimulus of their own kind. Before they begin to breed, however, their needs must be met—the parrots must be well fed, their surroundings must be clean and good health must be maintained.

The amount of light present seems to have an effect on the sexual activity of the bird. Increasing the light gradually from eight to twelve hours a day will encourage many species to breed. If natural sunlight is not available, you can obtain sunlight—simulating lights at your pet shop. In the wild parrots breed during the rainy season when there is more daylight and food is plentiful. In captivity, most breedings occur in spring and fall.

After the cage has been set up in a quiet area and the nest box attached, the birds can be placed in the cage. Food, water, oyster shell and many extras should be given to the breeders to keep them in top condition. Wheat bread soaked in milk, vitamins and alfalfa cubes can be added to the diet.

Sexual activity usually begins when the cock feeds the hen or vice versa to attract attention. In the writers' experience the matings take place in the morning or late at night, as also observed in the wild. The perches should not be loose, or proper mating will not occur and the eggs will be

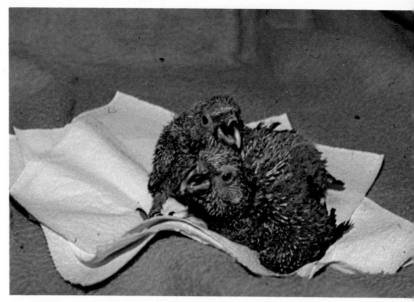

Shown above is a 27-day-old slender bill conure, while below are the same two chicks at 29 days of age. At this age the chicks are playful and very alert. Photos by Tony Silva.

At 31 days of age the slender bill chicks have a tail about 1½ inches long. At 42 days of age, they begin to test their wings and try to fly. Photos by Tony Silva.

infertile. Most conures will mate by keeping one foot on the perch and placing the other on the hen's back. Matings can occur several times a day. The hen might indicate she is ready for breeding by tossing shavings out of the box. The cock might assist her in doing this.

After mating, the hen spends long periods of time in the box. Her vent will start to bulge, and as time progresses the vent will become larger. This is the egg which will soon be laid. The eggs are generally laid every other day; sometimes there is a longer period between eggs. They are white and vary in size. After seven to eight days it should be assumed that those eggs that are clear are infertile. Do not remove these eggs, though. The eggs which show veins are developing and have an embryo. The incubation period for these eggs will vary between 24 to 26 days. A few days before the eggs are due to hatch, the hen will begin taking baths as mentioned previously. The humidity must be kept high. If all goes well, the chick will peck the shell with an eggtooth, which will later fall off. The eggshells will either be tossed out or eaten by the parents. The eggs which do not break open contain dead chicks or were infertile.

Most chicks are covered with a white down which will fall off later. Their development is slow; eyes will open a little at about eleven days, but are not fully open until much later. The pin feathers begin to emerge at about fourteen days on the wings and tail. It is a good idea to check the chicks daily and make notation of the weight and development. However, this cannot be done if the parents will not tolerate it. They might abandon the chicks or even kill them if they are disturbed.

Chicks must be kept warm and be fed within twelve hours of being hatched, or they will die. However, some parents will only feed those chicks which appear strong and lively. If a chick appears neglected, hungry or cold, it must be pulled and placed in an incubation box.

The female conure is the only one that incubates the

chicks. The male sits next to her for company and feeds the chicks after hatching. Even though some parents become very aggressive at this time, it is more important than ever to keep the cage clean and eating utensils thoroughly washed.

Incubators available for conures are the same type used for hatching poultry and quail eggs; they maintain the temperature and humidity at a constant level. Hatching the eggs in an incubator takes luck and practice, but it is very beneficial in case the parents become ill or will not care for the chicks.

Tame birds will breed just as well as wild ones. Such birds tend to be more aggressive since they have lost all fear of man, but nevertheless, they are good breeders. Some will come out to see their owner and leave their eggs and chicks, so it is important to spend as little time as possible with these birds. Some birds, such as macaws, will be lost as pets while breeding but will resume their pet personalities after breeding.

Employing foster parents in raising conures is common if the conures eat the eggs or refuse to feed the chicks. The eggs of some conures are the same size as those of cockatiels, and cockatiels often serve as foster parents. The eggs or chicks are given to a pair of cockatiels which have proved to be good feeders and raisers of young. The cockatiels are left to care for the chicks until they are a week old. At this time they are pulled for hand-feeding.

There are several reasons for pulling the chicks at birth, such as the parents refusing to feed the chicks or losing interest in them. Often the birds will nest again when the chicks or eggs are taken.

The chicks should be kept in an incubation box at 96 degrees F. If they pant or act uncomfortable, the temperature should be lowered a few degrees. However, if it is not kept warm enough, the chicks will not be able to digest their food and they may die.

Shown above, the slender bill conures play with a Senegal raised by the Haslingers. Below are the 70-day-old slender bill chicks. Photos in this series by Tony Silva.

A sun conure chick, shown above, will look like the birds below sitting in the sunshine when it is fully mature. Photo by P. Leyser.

The first feeding given to a chick should consist of plain monkey chow mixed with fresh bird droppings (from parents) or human saliva. This is used to begin building a fauna growth in the stomach. The following is a food formula for feeding the chicks:

1 lb. Purina Hi-Protein Monkey Chow
1 lb. hulled sunflower seed
½ lb. dry mynah pellets
¼ lb. Hi-Protein baby cereal.

Only the amount needed for one feeding should be mixed with hot water to a thin consistency. An eye dropper should be used to feed this formula. As the chicks grow older, baby vegetables and mashed fruit can be added to the formula.

Feedings should be given every two hours for the first seven days and two of the daily feedings should have calcium and vitamins added. The chicks should not be overfed since some of the food might go into the lungs and suffocate the bird. It is best to place the chick on a tissue in a small bowl for feeding and check the droppings carefully. After the first week, feed the chicks every two hours during the day and four hours during the night. By the fourteenth day, the chicks can be fed every four hours during the day and every five hours at night.

The chicks are kept in separate cups in the incubator box, but by the fifteenth day they can be grouped together. When handling a chick, be careful not to push its leg out of joint. The chick can go into shock and die. If a defective leg is detected, it can be tied loosely with yarn. Most bands can be put on a bird safely by the eighteenth day.

The crop of the chick should always be filled, but as the chick gets older, the crop could be allowed to empty once during the night. As the growing chicks get hungry, they become active. Soon the chicks will begin losing weight and start flying. At this stage it is best to keep the crop half full. If the bird regurgitates, it should be fed again. Seeds and pieces of fruit are now offered, and the chick will learn to

Sometimes during the handfeeding session your conure might become so covered with feed that you might have to bathe him. Do it carefully and keep him wrapped in a warm towel until he dries out.

crack seeds. Once this point is reached, the bird should be fed twice during the day and once before bedtime to be sure it has a full stomach.

If an incubator is not used for the chicks, a fish tank can be substituted after most of the chick's pin feathers have broken. Pine shavings should be used to a depth of four inches. Then newspaper can be added so the chicks can learn to walk.

The chick should be weighed daily on a gram scale while hand-feeding to be certain it has enough nourishment. If the bird gets a sour crop, stop feeding and work the food in the crop with a finger. Give the chick a bit of salt water. The food mixture must be kept thin until the chick becomes clear.

Some breeders sell their chicks before they can eat on their own. The disadvantage of this is that if there is a problem with the chick, the new owner might not be able to detect it. Be safe rather than sorry, and introduce the chick to a new environment when it has finished hand-feeding.

Sick birds (left) will look puffed and have loose droppings. This white-eyed conure is suffering from enteritis. The bird shown below is being examined to determine its state of health. Photos by Tony Silva and Barbara Kotlar.

First
Aid

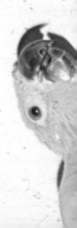

Most conures are healthy and hardy birds. This makes them ideal for beginning bird fanciers. However, the owner should always observe the physical characteristics and behavior of his bird. Many birds show no outward sign of being sick until they are beyond help. Consequently, most birds die from diseases and not old age as many believe. The following are some signs of a sick bird:

1. The bird will not eat.
2. There is discharge from nostrils or mouth.
3. The head is tucked under the wing or rump.
4. Diarrhea or very loose and watery droppings are present.
5. Weight loss is observed. Often the chest bone sticks out.
6. Large amounts of water are being consumed to prevent dehydration.

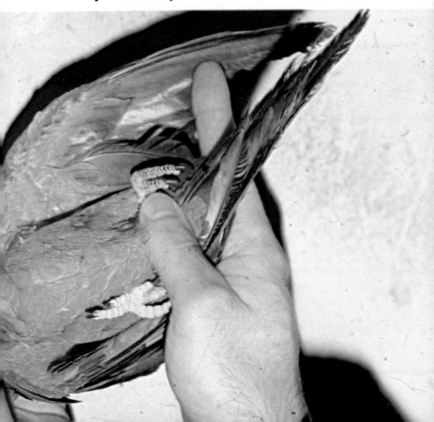

7. Breathing is labored, with the bird opening and closing its mouth. Often wheezing is present.
8. The bird is listless, perhaps even sitting on the bottom of the cage.
9. Growths are noticed around the beak.
10. The bird will sit low on its perch, covering its feet to keep warm.
11. The bird will stop talking.

The following are some of the disorders and diseases the bird might encounter.

INJURIES

If the conure is badly frightened and flies into the side of the cage or flight, it runs the risk of seriously injuring itself. Many are momentarily stunned, but if the force of impact is great enough, the neck of the bird might be broken and the bird will die almost instantly. Prevention of occurences such as this should be a prime concern of the bird fancier.

Broken legs and wings are other possible injuries: however, they are best left alone. A splint is ideal in treating broken legs, but it would soon end up in pieces since it is annoying to the bird. The legs and wings will heal soon by themselves although there might be some disfigurement evident. If complete severing occurs, take the bird to a vet since this is a very serious situation. Keep the perch close to the bottom of the cage to discourage climbing and keep the cage partially covered to provide a safe haven for the bird.

TUMORS

Tumors which can occur in aging conures may appear anywhere on the body, but the chest and throat are likely spots. Many are fatty tumors which might not pose a threat to the life of the bird; however, cancerous tumors can develop in birds from time to time. They cannot be treated and are eventually fatal to the bird. Again seek out the advice of a qualified veterinarian if a tumor is present. He can decide if removal is necessary or if an operation would be detrimental to the bird's health.

ENTERITIS

This is a disease that affects birds that are kept in a dirty, crowded area. There are actually two types of enteritis—one is contagious and the other isn't. Symptoms include diarrhea, swelling of the abdomen, loss of weight and rapid breathing. It is necessary to keep the bird warm and isolated from other birds, and a vet should be notified immediately since this disease can be fatal.

It should be mentioned that anyone who has an aviary or even just one caged bird should take precautions in protecting their birds from unneccessary exposure to diseases such as enteritis. Bird fanciers always enjoy observing birds in zoos and pet shops, but in some instances the birds can be sick or carrying a disease that can be detrimental to other birds. If a person touches a bird or cage in these places, hands should be washed before handling other birds. The authors feel that even clothing and shoes should be changed if there is the slightest possibility that germs or viruses might be carried back to the aviary.

CANDIDIASIS

This disease is caused by a fungus, *Candida albicans,* and can be induced by long periods of treatment with antibiotics. A white growth similar to cottage cheese forms inside the mouth. The bird will at times breathe by opening and closing the mouth. It is actually suffocating. Treatment consists of giving the bird two doses daily of vitamin A which is available at pet shops. The bird should also be fed raw vegetables which are high in this vitamin. After three days there should be a noticeable improvement. To keep the bird on a maintenance program, sprinkle cod-liver oil on its fruit and vegetables daily. Do not let this food spoil, or it will cause diarrhea.

The red rump on this janday conure is normal. On the facing page, the top photo shows specimens of the nanday conure, while the lower photo shows sun conures. Photos by Tony Silva and Dr. Herbert R. Axelrod.

SCALY FEET

Mites or old age can cause scales to grow on the feet. Vaseline or an ointment specifically sold for this purpose in pet shops should be applied daily. After several days improvement should be noticed.

COLDS

Colds are very common in caged birds. Causes could be a drop in room temperature or a cold draft. Symptoms are very much like those of a human cold, and often the bird stops eating. The bird must be kept warm and treated as soon as possible. An antibiotic should be given. Often medication is stopped as soon as the bird looks better, but it is advised to give the bird the recommended dosage for a full seven days so the cold will not reappear.

FEATHER PLUCKING

This problem is common in parrot-type birds. The bird will attempt to pick every feather on the body, wings and tail. Often boredom and neglect prompt this habit. Attention and a well-balanced diet with plenty of seeds available might prove to be beneficial.

Some birds will pluck for so long that the feathers will stop coming in. Such feather pickers can be used for breeding with success, but many will pick their babies while in the nest.

Do not assume that because a few feathers are found at the bottom of the cage the bird is a picker. It could be molting. Another possibility is that the bird is in breeding condition; if offered a mate, it will stop picking.

There is also a product on the market made from aloe that is used for quail and poultry. It has been used effectively on parrots, and if applied weekly for a month, the problem can clear. A collar around the neck made of cardboard or heavy plastic in the shape of a funnel can protect the bird from itself if all else fails.

FEATHER ROT

This disorder is more common in cockatoos, but it can also occur in conures. The feathering on the bird is dry and dull, and the feathers never develop properly. Most fall off while still encased in the sheath covering feathers. The disease can be caused by a dietary deficiency, so a balanced diet is essential in maintaining good health. Two drops of iodine should be added to the water twice weekly.

RED EYE

Red eye, a condition in which the tissue around the eye becomes red and swollen, is common in imported cockatiels and *Neophema* parrakeets. Dirty perches can be a cause. Yellow mercury of oxide (2% solution) available at drug stores or a medicated powder sold especially for this problem at pet shops should be given twice daily until the inflammation subsides. Follow the directions on the medication.

WORMS

Worms rarely occur in birds, but when they are present birds will show signs of being ill, while continuing to eat. Usually the bird will contract this in the wild, not in captivity. A remedy that the Indians of the Caribbean use is to squeeze the milk out of the meat of a coconut and give this to the bird. Usually, within a week, the bird will pass the worms.

PACHECO'S PARROT DISEASE

Until recently Pacheco's parrot disease was almost unheard of in the United States bird market. It was first discovered in Brazil fifty years ago, and it has been brought in by South American parrots. Conures seem to have a natural immunity, which leads some to believe they are carriers, especially the Patagonian and nanday. Recently a vaccine was developed with funding by the International Bird Institute, and it will soon be available.

This disease only affects parrots. It is spread by contact, not through the air. Birds become infected after being in

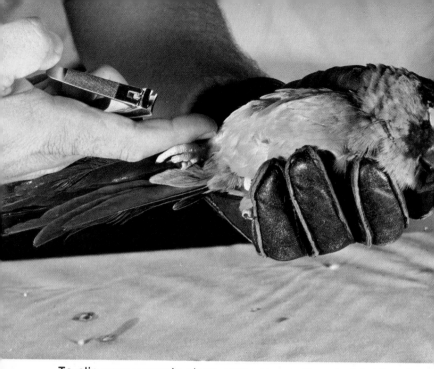

To clip your conure's claws, wear gloves. Then isolate the claw (below) and clip it very carefully near the tip. Photos by Dr. Herbert R. Axelrod.

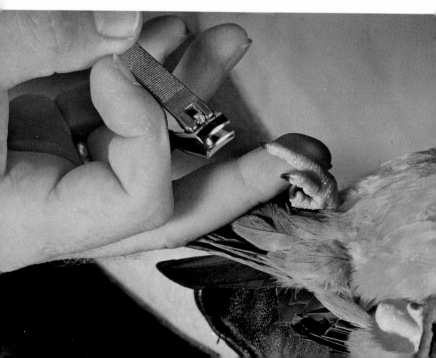

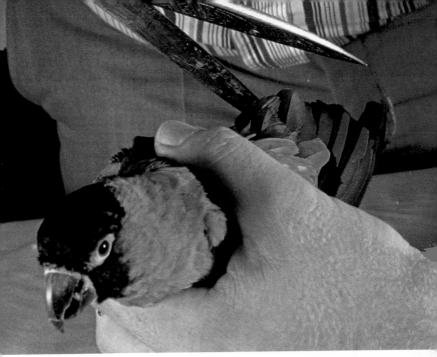

Use scissors to cut the bird's wings, but not the way shown above. Hold the wing out (below) and cut off the ends of all of the primary feathers. Here two primaries have not been cut yet. Photos by Dr. Herbert R. Axelrod.

direct contact and by using eating and drinking utensils of sick birds.

If the disease is present, everything should be thoroughly cleaned with a disinfectant and the infected bird removed. The owner should keep his hands scrupulously clean and change his clothing to halt the spread of the disease.

A bird usually shows no signs of having the disease until it is too late, although sometimes there is some loss of control of the body and nasal discharge. The disease can be detected by fluoroscopic analysis. A postmortem shows lesions and white spots on the liver, which is enlarged and pale in color.

ORNITHOSIS

This disease affects all birds, not only parrots. Detecting ornithosis and exotic Newcastle disease is the reason why birds are quarantined before entering the country. The organism *Chlamydia* is the underlying cause of ornithosis. If a bird has the disease, it will stop eating and slowly waste away. The disease is cured with a thirty-day treatment of chlorotetracycline which is placed in a mash of cooked corn. The chances of humans contracting ornithosis are slim.

OVERGROWN BEAKS

This problem is common in older captive birds. Birds in the wild are constantly chewing and climbing, wearing down their beaks and nails. A bird whose beak is overgrown should have it clipped back and have plenty of twigs and branches available for chewing. The beak can be cut or filed down for a normal appearance.

MOLTING

Birds molt; that is, they replace feathers normally about every six months. Birds that have bad feathering should be allowed to molt naturally; however, if the owner desires the bird to molt prematurely, the process can be hastened by keeping the bird warm and pulling a few tail feathers.

This halfmoon conure has an overgrown beak which requires trimming. The best way to trim the beak is with a file or emery board.

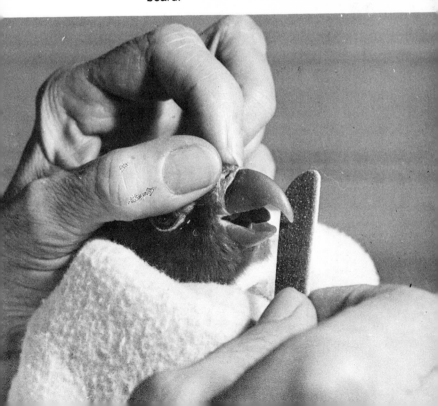

Small cages are usually not recommended for conures that require exercise, but they are excellent as carrying cages if you must travel with your bird or as a hospital cage if your bird must be restrained.

Even experts wearing gloves sometimes get bitten. Dr. Matthew Vriends didn't pose for this picture, it just happened. Photos by Dr. Herbert R. Axelrod.

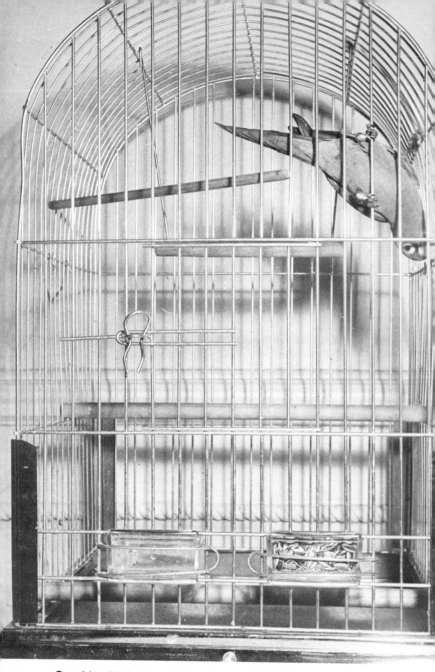

Good health begins with good sanitary conditions for your bird. If your cage is dirty, if the water is filthy and if the seed is moldy, you can expect a sick bird to result.

Spray the bird daily while molting. This will encourage the bird to preen its feathers. If a bird has a clipped wing, the feathers will come back in at six months after a molt.

One should never cut a pin feather which is encased in a sheath that is just growing. If this feather is cut, it will bleed. If one is broken by a bird, pull it to prevent excess blood loss. It is advisable to allow someone who is knowledgeable in birds to handle this situation.

DIARRHEA

Diarrhea can have many causes. It could indicate a serious disorder or a mild upset, such as a reaction to a newly introduced fruit or vegetable. Often nervous birds or ones placed in new surroundings will get it. Lettuce will sometimes cause a digestive upset. If the bird has a soupy green, yellow, black or any other unnaturally colored stool, it should be taken to a veterinarian where a culture of the stool can be taken. If blood is present, this could point to an injury in the intestinal wall. Call a veterinarian immediately.

CARE FOR SICK BIRDS

When a veterinarian is not available, a sick bird should be kept warm (90-95° F). If not kept at this temperature the bird will use its chest muscles as fuel to stay warm. A fish tank can be used to hold a sick bird: cover the top with mesh screening and place a 100-watt lamp above it to maintain heat. Newspaper should be used on the bottom of the tank, and droppings should be checked several times a day. Do not give the bird a perch. It is better for the bird to sit puffed up on the bottom of the tank so it doesn't use much body fuel.

The bird should be encouraged to eat frequently, for a bird cannot go for long without food. Offer the bird all its favorite treats. If the bird is weak but hungry, give it seed that has been soaked. The seed should be washed thoroughly, placed in water and put in the refrigerator for 24 to 36 hours. Rinse the seed again when it is taken out. Soaked seed is easier for the bird to digest and less difficult to crack.

A friendly conure whose beak badly needs trimming lands on the head of its pal, a boxer. Photo by Sam Fehrenz. On the facing page is a friendly nanday conure. Photo by Dr. Herbert R. Axelrod.

If the bird is tame, all effort should be made to hand-feed it. Monkey chow, honey and peanut butter can be taken by many birds. Give it as much as it will take. If the bird is tame but refuses to eat, place a few drops of honey water (50/50) in its mouth with an eye dropper. If more is given, the liquid can go into the lungs and suffocate the bird. Do not attempt to tube-feed a bird (feeding a bird directly in its crop with a tube). Even experienced people have lost birds by this method.

It is best to give the bird medicine by using an eye dropper and placing it directly into the bird's mouth. The amount of medicine actually given to the bird is easier to keep track of this way. Do not spare any attempt in trying to save the bird!

Some owners take their birds for a yearly check-up. This is only feasible if there are a few birds kept as pets. Seek out a qualified veterinarian who has experience with birds.

When this Jamaican conure began to shed its feathers (facing page), act listless and sit and excrete into its feed dish, the bird had to be removed and placed into a hospital cage (below) for careful observation. A large aquarium with a screen cover is a perfect hospital cage if one is available. Photos by Dr. Herbert R. Axelrod.